Girls For The Win!
Girls on the FIELD HOCKEY TEAM

Beth Gottlieb

Enslow PUBLISHING

DISCOVER!

Please visit our website, www.enslow.com. For a free color catalog of all our high-quality books, call toll free 1-800-398-2504 or fax 1-877-980-4454.

Library of Congress Cataloging-in-Publication Data
Names: Gottlieb, Beth, author.
Title: Girls on the field hockey team / Beth Gottlieb.
Description: New York, N.Y. : Enslow Publishing, [2023] | Series: Girls for the win! | Includes bibliographical references and index.
Identifiers: LCCN 2021043671 (print) | LCCN 2021043672 (ebook) | ISBN 9781978528079 (set) | ISBN 9781978528086 (library binding) | ISBN 9781978528062 (paperback) | ISBN 9781978528093 (ebook)
Subjects: LCSH: Field hockey–Juvenile literature.
Classification: LCC GV1017.H7 G67 2023 (print) | LCC GV1017.H7 (ebook) | DDC 796.355–dc23
LC record available at https://lccn.loc.gov/2021043671
LC ebook record available at https://lccn.loc.gov/2021043672

Published in 2023 by
Enslow Publishing
29 E. 21st Street
New York, NY 10010

Copyright © 2023 Enslow Publishing

Designer: Katelyn E. Reynolds
Interior Design: Tanya Dellaccio
Editor: Kristen Nelson

Photo credits: Cover (girl) Madelein Wolfaardt/Shutterstock.com; series background (stars) LHF Graphics/Shutterstock.com; series background (notepad) BeatWalk/Shutterstock.com; field hockey stick andrykay/Shutterstock.com; series background (wood grain) Anucha Tiemsom/Shutterstock.com; series background (highlighter) CRStocker/Shutterstock.com; p. 5 SpeedKingz/Shutterstock.com; p. 7 Juice Flair/Shutterstock.com; p. 9 StockphotoVideo/Shutterstock.com; p. 11 Courtesy of the Library of Congress; pp. 13 (main image), 17 Skumer/Shutterstock.com; p. 13 (field hockey stick) MH STOCK/Shutterstock.com; p. 15 Prixel Creative/Shutterstock.com; p. 19 Corepics VOF/Shutterstock.com; p. 21 https://upload.wikimedia.org/wikipedia/commons/4/47/Lucha_Aymar.jpg.

Portions of this work were originally authored by David Anthony and published as *Girls Play Field Hockey*. All new material this edition authored by Beth Gottlieb.

All rights reserved. No part of this book may be reproduced in any form without permission in writing from the publisher, except by a reviewer.

Printed in the United States of America

Some of the images in this book illustrate individuals who are models. The depictions do not imply actual situations or events.

CPSIA compliance information: Batch #CSENS23: For further information contact Enslow Publishing, New York, New York, at 1-800-398-2504.

CONTENTS

Get on the Field!. 4
Just Hockey 8
Hockey History 10
Game Basics 12
Goalie and Gear 16
College and Beyond 18
Words to Know 22
For More Information 23
Index. 24

Boldface words appear in Words to Know.

GET ON THE FIELD!

Whether on a school field or **turf** at the **Olympics**, girls all over the world play field hockey. It's a fast-paced team sport in which players must work together. In the United States, field hockey is played mainly by girls and women in high school and **college**.

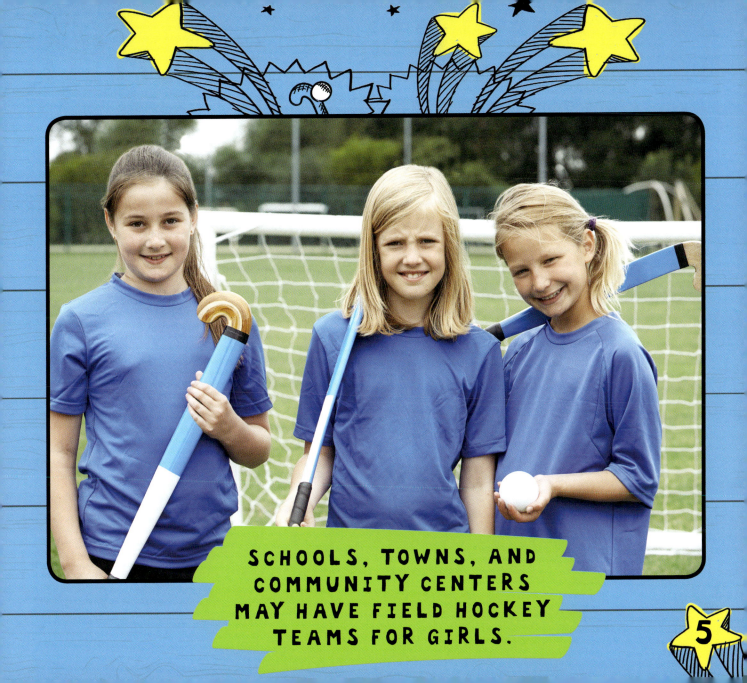
SCHOOLS, TOWNS, AND COMMUNITY CENTERS MAY HAVE FIELD HOCKEY TEAMS FOR GIRLS.

Field hockey is a game played with a stick and a ball. It's most often played on grass or artificial, or fake, turf. Field hockey can be played outdoors with 11 players per team. It can be played indoors with six players per team.

IN OTHER PARTS OF THE WORLD, BOTH MEN AND WOMEN PLAY FIELD HOCKEY IN ABOUT EQUAL NUMBERS.

JUST HOCKEY

Field hockey is just called "hockey" in most countries. However, its full name is most often used in the United States and Canada. In these countries, another kind of hockey—ice hockey—is very popular.

The National Women's Hockey **League** is a **professional** ice hockey league for women in the United States. It started in 2015.

Hockey History

The first women's field hockey club was founded in 1887. Constance Applebee introduced field hockey to women in the United States in 1901. She showed women at Harvard University how to play. After that, field hockey was played by women at other U.S. colleges.

UNTIL THE LATE 1800S, ONLY MEN WERE ALLOWED TO PLAY FIELD HOCKEY.

GAME BASICS

Field hockey players aim to score points by shooting the ball into the other team's goal using their stick. Each goal is worth one point. Players use small taps of the stick to move the ball down the field.

FIELD HOCKEY PLAYERS CAN'T USE THEIR FEET TO SCORE OR TO MOVE THE BALL DOWN THE FIELD.

FIELD HOCKEY STICK AND BALL

Field hockey teams have **offensive** players called forwards and **defensive** players called fullbacks. A forward works to score goals. A fullback works to stop the other team from scoring. A midfielder both helps her team score and helps stop the other team from scoring.

FIELD HOCKEY GAMES ARE CALLED MATCHES. THEY ARE OFTEN BROKEN INTO TWO HALVES THAT ARE EACH 35 MINUTES LONG.

OUTDOOR FIELD HOCKEY POSITIONS

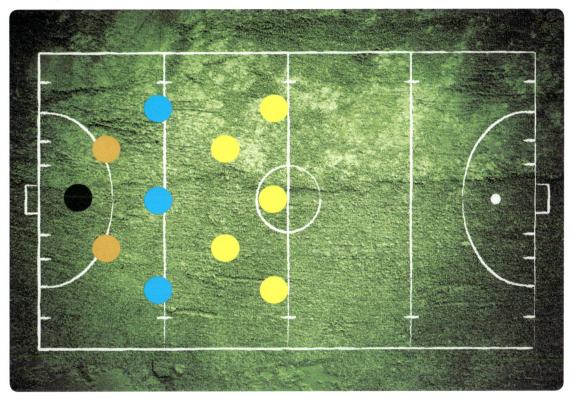

- 🟡 FORWARD
- 🔵 MIDFIELDER
- 🟠 FULLBACK
- ⚫ GOALIE

GOALIE AND GEAR

A goalkeeper's job is to stop the ball from going in the goal. She can use her feet and other body parts to do this. Goalkeepers wear special safety gear. It includes a helmet, a chest **protector**, and many pads.

THE GOALIE WEARS SAFETY GEAR TO PROTECT HER FROM THE FAST SHOTS THAT COME AT HER.

COLLEGE AND BEYOND

If you work hard in school and on the field, you could play field hockey in college. The best field hockey players in the world face each other every four years in the Women's Hockey World Cup. It first occurred in 1974.

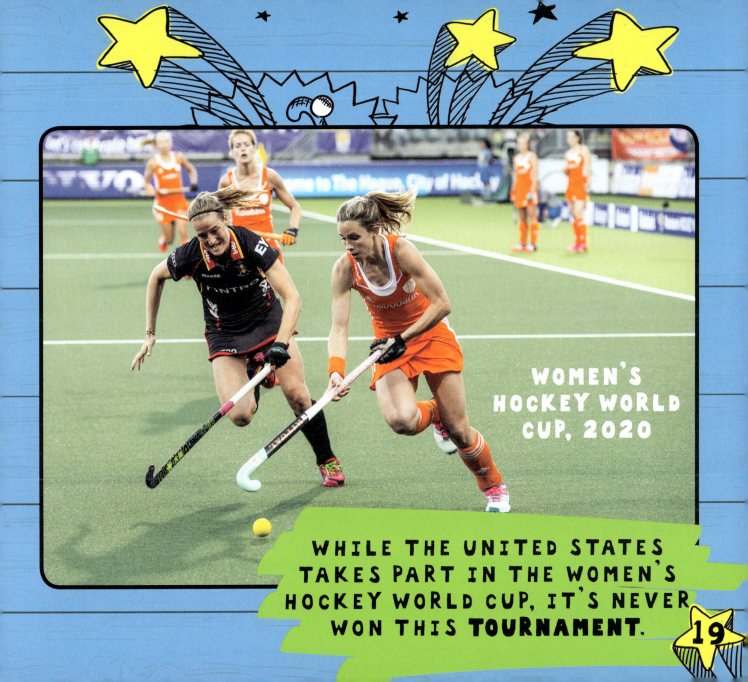

WOMEN'S HOCKEY WORLD CUP, 2020

WHILE THE UNITED STATES TAKES PART IN THE WOMEN'S HOCKEY WORLD CUP, IT'S NEVER WON THIS **TOURNAMENT**.

19

Field hockey is a popular sport at the Summer Olympics. Women's field hockey became part of the Olympics in 1980. The U.S. women's field hockey team won a bronze **medal** at the 1984 Olympics, which were held in Los Angeles, California.

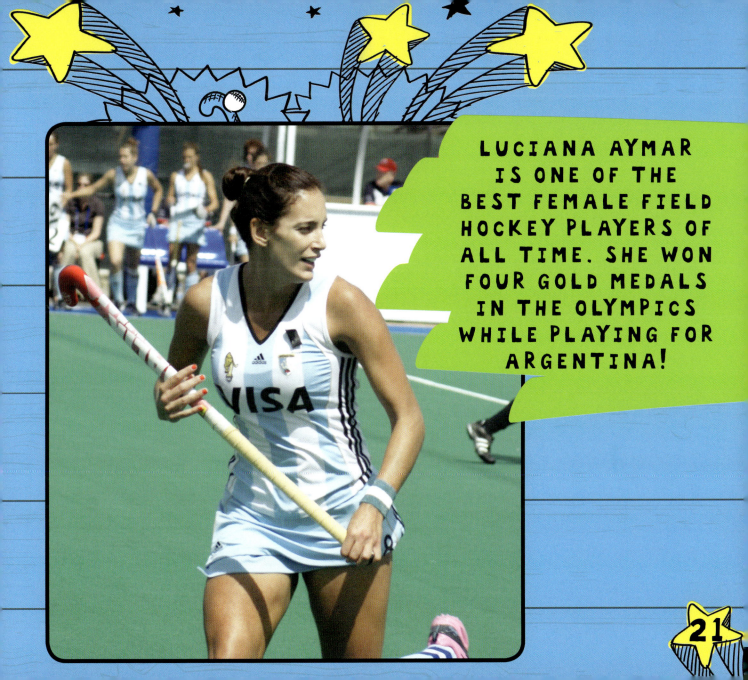

Words to Know

college A school after high school.
defensive Having to do with the defense, or the part of a team trying to stop another team from scoring points.
league A group of teams that play the same sport and compete against each other.
medal A flat, small piece of metal with art or words that's used as an honor or reward.
offensive Having to do with the offense, or the part of a team trying to score points.
Olympics A series of international athletic contests held in a different country once every four years.
professional Having to do with a job someone does for a living.
protector Something that keeps someone or something safe.
tournament A series of contests testing the skill of many athletes in the same sport.
turf The thick mat of artificial grass used for playing fields.

For More Information

Books

Dufresne, Emilie. *Field Hockey*. New York, NY: Kidhaven Publishing, 2020.

Duling, Kaitlyn. *Women in Hockey*. Lake Elmo, MN: Focus Readers, 2020.

Websites

Rules
girlsfieldhockey.org/rules/
Review the basic rules of field hockey here.

USA Field Hockey Futures
www.teamusa.org/usa-field-hockey/futures
Do you want to play field hockey in the Olympics? Check out the futures program!

Publisher's note to educators and parents: Our editors have carefully reviewed these websites to ensure that they are suitable for students. Many websites change frequently, however, and we cannot guarantee that a site's future contents will continue to meet our high standards of quality and educational value. Be advised that students should be closely supervised whenever they access the internet.

INDEX

Applebee, Constance, 10
Aymar, Luciana, 21
ball, 6, 12
Canada, 8
college, 4, 10, 18
forward, 14
fullback, 14
goalie, 16, 17
gear, 16
Harvard University, 10
ice hockey, 8, 9
indoor, 6
midfielder, 14
National Women's Hockey League, 9
Olympics, 4, 20, 21
outdoor, 6
stick, 6, 12
turf, 4, 6
United States, 4, 8, 9, 10, 19
Women's Hockey World Cup, 18, 19